MICHAEL PHELPS

★ OLYMPIC SWIMMER ★

KATIE LAJINESS

Big Buddy Books
An Imprint of Abdo Publishing
abdopublishing.com

BIG BUDDY OLYMPIC BIOGRAPHIES

abdopublishing.com

Published by Abdo Publishing, a division of ABDO, PO Box 398166, Minneapolis, Minnesota 55439.
Copyright © 2017 by Abdo Consulting Group, Inc. International copyrights reserved in all countries.
No part of this book may be reproduced in any form without written permission from the publisher.
Big Buddy Books™ is a trademark and logo of Abdo Publishing.

Printed in the United States of America, North Mankato, Minnesota.
102016
012017

THIS BOOK CONTAINS
RECYCLED MATERIALS

Cover Photo: PA Images/Alamy Stock Photo Interior Photos: Alireza
Interior Photos: ASSOCIATED PRESS (pp. 13, 15, 17, 19, 23, 25, 27, 31); dpa picture alliance/Alamy
    Stock Photo (p. 5); Invision for SUBWAY/AP (p. 6); PCN Photography/Alamy Stock Photo (p. 21);
    REUTERS/Alamy Stock Photo (pp. 9, 11); ZUMA Press, Inc./Alamy Stock Photo (p. 29).

Coordinating Series Editor: Tamara L. Britton
Graphic Design: Jenny Christensen

Publisher's Cataloging-in-Publication Data

Names: Lajiness, Katie, author.
Title: Michael Phelps / by Katie Lajiness.
Description: Minneapolis, MN : Abdo Publishing, 2017. | Series: Big buddy
    Olympic biographies | Includes bibliographical references and index.
Identifiers: LCCN 2016953142 | ISBN 9781680785555 (lib. bdg.) |
    ISBN 9781680785838 (ebook)
Subjects: LCSH: Phelps, Michael, 1985- --Juvenile literature. | Swimmers--
    United States--Biography--Juvenile literature. | Olympic athletes--
    United States--Biography--Juvenile literature. | Olympic Games (31st : 2016 :
    Rio de Janeiro, Brazil)
Classification: DDC 797.2/1092 [B]--dc23
LC record available at http://lccn.loc.gov/2016953142

CONTENTS

RECORD BREAKER

Michael Phelps is a famous swimmer. He won races at the Olympics, the FINA World **Championships**, and the Pan Pacific Championships.

Over five Olympics, Michael earned 28 **medals**. He has more Olympic medals than any other **athlete**.

SNAPSHOT

NAME:
Michael Fred Phelps II

BIRTHDAY:
June 30, 1985

BIRTHPLACE:
Baltimore, Maryland

TURNED PROFESSIONAL:
2001

OLYMPIC MEDALS WON:
23 gold, 3 silver, 2 bronze

CHAMPIONSHIPS:
FINA World Championships
and Pan Pacific

FAMILY TIES

Michael Fred Phelps II was born on June 30, 1985, in Baltimore, Maryland. His parents are Fred and Debbie Phelps. They divorced when he was nine. Michael has two older sisters named Hilary and Whitney.

Michael's sisters Whitney (*left*) and Hilary (*right*) are also swimmers.

WHERE IN THE WORLD?

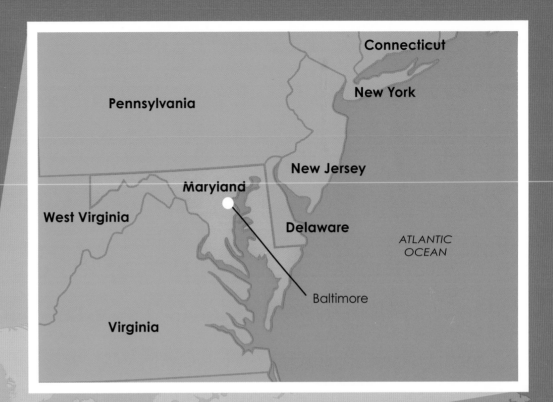

Connecticut

New York

Pennsylvania

New Jersey

Maryland

West Virginia

Delaware

ATLANTIC OCEAN

Baltimore

Virginia

N
W E
S

EARLY YEARS

Michael started swimming lessons at age seven. Three years later, he was a top US youth swimmer. When Michael was 11, he began training with **coach** Bob Bowman.

During elementary school, Michael learned he had **ADHD**. Daily swimming practices helped him deal with his condition.

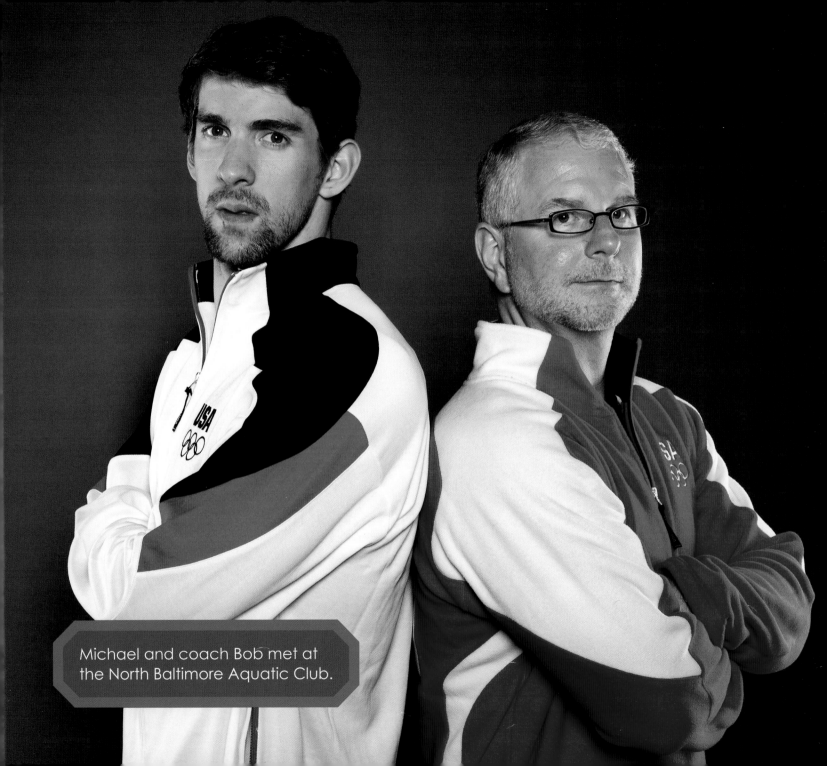

Michael and coach Bob met at the North Baltimore Aquatic Club.

STARTING OUT

In 2000, Michael traveled to Sydney, Australia, for his first Olympics. At 15, he was the youngest male swimmer on the US team. Sadly, Michael didn't win a **medal**.

Michael continued to train hard. In 2001, he became a **professional** swimmer. Michael could not **compete** in college sports, but he earned money from his swimming fame.

Michael is six feet five inches (2 m) tall. His wingspan is three inches (8 cm) longer than he is tall!

ATHENS OLYMPICS

By 2004, Michael was already a five-time world **champion**. But, he wanted to show people that he could do even better.

That chance came when Michael went to Athens, Greece, to **compete** in his second Olympics. He swam in six individual and two relay events. Michael earned six gold and two bronze **medals**.

Michael (*above center*) won a gold medal for the 400-meter individual medley. He set a new world record of 4:08.26 minutes.

BEIJING OLYMPICS

In 2008, Michael traveled to Beijing, China to **compete** in his third Olympics. Michael had high hopes. He wanted to become the first **athlete** to win eight gold **medals** at a single Olympics.

Michael had a tough schedule. He had 17 races in nine days. But Michael struck gold and broke records in his first three events.

Michael has mastered all four competitive swimming strokes. They are the backstroke, the breaststroke (*shown*), the butterfly, and the freestyle.

During the 200-meter butterfly, Michael's goggles filled with water. He couldn't see well. But, he still won the race and set another record!

By the end of the Beijing Olympics, Michael broke seven world records and one Olympic record. And he reached his goal of winning eight gold **medals**. This set a new Olympic record!

Brendan Hansen (*left*), Michael (*second from left*), Aaron Peirsol (*second from right*), and Jason Lezak (*right*) won gold in the 4x100 relay. They helped set a world record of 3:08.24 minutes.

LONDON OLYMPICS

After his success in Beijing, Michael had nothing to prove. He was the greatest swimmer in history! But he wasn't done yet.

In 2012, Michael **competed** in his fourth Olympics. In London, England, Michael won four gold and two silver **medals**. With a total of 22 medals, he was the winningest **athlete** in Olympic history.

Michael is known for wearing two swim caps. Two caps help keep his goggles on during a race.

In total, more than 2,100 medals were won in London.

19

RIO OLYMPICS

Michael took a break from swimming after the London Olympics. Then in 2014, he decided to start training again. Some people questioned whether Michael could **compete** in his fifth Olympics. But Michael trained harder than ever before.

DID YOU KNOW?
Michael has earned more medals than 90 different countries.

Michael won the 200-meter butterfly in 1:54.12 minutes.

The 2016 Olympics were held in Rio de Janeiro, Brazil. Michael, at age 31, swam in six events. His hard work from the past two years paid off. Michael won a **medal** in all six races! He had a total of 28 Olympic medals, 23 of which were gold.

DID YOU KNOW?
Michael is the first US swimmer to appear in five Olympics.

Michael has won a gold medal in the 200-meter individual medley in four straight Olympics. This is a record!

MICHAEL PHELPS FOUNDATION

Michael uses his fame to help others. In 2008, he started the Michael Phelps **Foundation**. This group teaches swimming skills and the benefits of healthy living.

In 2015, Michael met young swimmers at a swim club in Knoxville, Tennessee.

OUT OF THE WATER

Michael is famous all over the world. He **promotes** products for many companies. And, he has appeared on magazine covers and TV shows.

Michael is one of the most well-known Olympic athletes. He has written books and appeared on cereal boxes.

BUZZ

After the Rio Olympics, Michael **retired** from **professional** swimming. But, he won't be far from the pool. Michael will be a **coach** at Arizona State University in Tempe, Arizona. Fans are excited to see what's next for Michael Phelps!

Michael plans to spend time with his fiancée Nicole and their son Boomer.

GLOSSARY

ADHD attention deficit/hyperactivity disorder. A condition in which a person has trouble paying attention, sitting still, or controlling actions.

athlete a person who is trained or skilled in sports.

championship a game, a match, or a race held to find a first-place winner. A champion is someone who wins a championship.

coach someone who teaches or trains a person or a group on a certain subject or skill.

compete to take part in a contest between two or more persons or groups.

foundation (faun-DAY-shuhn) an organization that controls gifts of money and services.

medal an award for success.

professional (pruh-FEHSH-nuhl) paid to do a sport or activity.

promote to help something become known.

retire to give up one's job.

WEBSITES

To learn more about Olympic Biographies, visit **booklinks.abdopublishing.com**. These links are routinely monitored and updated to provide the most current information available.

INDEX